FAVORITE BRAND NAME

Family Favorites

A Classic Recipe Collection

Publications International, Ltd.

Recipe Development: Lynn Foley, The Lipton Kitchens

Photography: Sacco Studio Limited, Chicago
Photographer: Tom O'Connell
Photo Stylist: Melissa J. Frisco
Production: Melinda R. Sacco
Food Stylists: Tobe LeMoine, Walter Moeller, Josephine Orba
Assistant Food Stylist: Liza Brown

Pictured on the front cover: Lasagna Florentine *(page 32)*.
Pictured on the back cover *(clockwise from top left):* Classic Stuffed Shells *(page 30),* Summer Minestrone with Pesto *(page 76)* and Roasted Garlic Parmesan Penne Primavera *(page 52).*

ISBN: 0-7853-3377-0

Manufactured in U.S.A.

8 7 6 5 4 3 2 1

Nutritional Analysis: Nutritional information is given for some of the recipes in this publication. Each analysis is based on the food items in the ingredient list, except ingredients labeled as "optional" or "for garnish." When more than one ingredient choice is listed, the first ingredient is used for analysis. If a range for the amount of an ingredient is given, the nutritional analysis is based on the lowest amount. Foods offered as "serve with" suggestions are not included in the analysis unless otherwise stated.

Microwave Cooking: Microwave ovens vary in wattage. Use the cooking times as guidelines and check for doneness before adding more time.

Family Favorites

A Classic Recipe Collection

TABLE OF CONTENTS

From Our Family to Yours

Come in, grab a plate, join us!

*Y*ou're invited to savor the exciting recipes we've developed with your family in mind. For over 60 years, Ragú® has been a favorite with great families like yours. We make irresistible sauces that help you make terrific meals. Ragú varieties are made with the best ingredients such as vine-ripened tomatoes, onions, zesty garlic, Romano cheese and the perfect blend of herbs and spices.

Ragú offers Old World Style®, the original, for those who prefer a smooth, mild classic Italian sauce; Chunky Gardenstyle which comes full of vegetable goodness; Hearty Robust Blend with distinctive, full flavor sauces; and Light with sumptuous low-fat and fat-free varieties. And don't forget our newest sauce...Cheese Creations!™ made with real cheese and no preservatives. For another fine Italian meal, feast on pizza with Pizza Quick® Sauce. Whatever your preferred style, you can customize each recipe with your family's favorite flavor. We have over 25 delicious flavors in all!

Our cookbook features 60 mouthwatering quick and easy recipes. For those hectic weeknights, try our fuss-free favorites. When the weekend rolls around, gather the family around the table to enjoy our Sunday supper specials complete with super snacks and side dishes. There are also recipes on the lighter side that are anything but light on taste. Your friends will be delighted with our special entertaining recipes. And we've got kid-pleasing meals that are as much fun to make as they are to eat.

So let Ragú help you make your mealtime a time to celebrate with your family!

RAGÚ®

Weeknight Wonders

Three Cheese Baked Ziti (page 10)

Three Cheese Baked Ziti

Makes 8 servings

1 container (15 ounces) part-skim ricotta cheese
2 eggs, beaten
¼ cup grated Parmesan cheese
1 box (16 ounces) ziti pasta, cooked and drained
1 jar (28 ounces) Ragú® Chunky Gardenstyle
    Pasta Sauce
1 cup shredded mozzarella cheese (about
    4 ounces)

Preheat oven to 350°F. In large bowl, combine ricotta cheese, eggs and Parmesan cheese; set aside.

In another bowl, thoroughly combine pasta and Ragú Chunky Gardenstyle Pasta Sauce.

In 13×9-inch baking dish, spoon ½ of the pasta mixture; evenly top with ricotta cheese mixture, then remaining pasta mixture. Sprinkle with mozzarella cheese. Bake 30 minutes or until heated through. Serve, if desired, with additional heated pasta sauce.

Sausage & Chicken-Stuffed Pita Sandwiches

Makes 6 servings

¾ pound Italian sausage links, sliced
¾ pound boneless, skinless chicken breasts,
    cut into ¾-inch cubes
1 clove garlic, finely chopped
1½ cups Ragú Old World Style® Pasta Sauce
1 cup shredded mozzarella cheese (about
    4 ounces)
6 large pita breads, heated

Preheat oven to 350°F. In 12-inch nonstick skillet, cook sausage over medium-high heat, stirring occasionally, 5 minutes. Add chicken and garlic and cook, stirring occasionally, 5 minutes. Stir in Ragú Old World Style Pasta Sauce and simmer uncovered 5 minutes or until sausage is done and chicken is no longer pink. Remove from heat; stir in cheese. To serve, generously stuff pita bread with sausage mixture. Garnish, if desired, with grated Parmesan cheese.

RECIPE TIP

The quickest way to peel garlic is to press each clove with the flat side of a knife until the paper-like skin breaks; the skin slips off easily.

Chicken & Creamy Garlic Sauce

Makes 4 servings

1 teaspoon olive or vegetable oil
4 boneless, skinless chicken breast halves
1 jar (17 ounces) Ragú® Cheese Creations!™
   Roasted Garlic Parmesan Pasta Sauce
1 small tomato, chopped
8 ounces rotelle pasta, cooked and drained

In 12-inch nonstick skillet, heat oil over medium heat and lightly brown chicken. Stir in Ragú Cheese Creations! Pasta Sauce and tomato. Simmer covered, stirring occasionally, 10 minutes or until chicken is no longer pink. To serve, spoon chicken and sauce over hot pasta. Garnish, if desired, with crisp-cooked crumbled bacon and chopped fresh basil.

Skillet Pasta Dinner

Makes 4 servings

1 pound ground beef
1 jar (28 ounces) Ragú® Hearty Robust Blend
   Pasta Sauce
8 ounces rotini pasta, cooked and drained
1 cup shredded cheddar cheese, divided
2 teaspoons chili powder (optional)

In 12-inch skillet, brown ground beef over medium-high heat; drain. Stir in Ragú Hearty Robust Blend Pasta Sauce, hot pasta, ¾ cup cheese and chili powder. Simmer uncovered, stirring occasionally, 5 minutes or until heated through. Sprinkle with remaining ¼ cup cheese.

*Chicken & Creamy
Garlic Sauce*

Cheese Tortellini in Tomato Cream Sauce

Makes 4 servings

1 jar (28 ounces) Ragú® Chunky Gardenstyle Pasta Sauce
⅓ cup whipping or heavy cream
¼ cup grated Parmesan cheese
½ teaspoon salt
⅛ teaspoon cayenne pepper
1 package (15 ounces) cheese tortellini
1 box (10 ounces) frozen peas

In 12-inch skillet, combine Ragú Chunky Gardenstyle Pasta Sauce, cream, Parmesan cheese, salt and cayenne pepper. Simmer uncovered, stirring occasionally, until heated through.

Meanwhile, cook tortellini according to package directions, adding peas during last 1 minute of cooking; drain. Toss tortellini and peas with hot sauce.

RECIPE TIP

Feel free to substitute ravioli or your favorite pasta for the tortellini, if desired.

Cheese Tortellini in Tomato Cream Sauce

Spicy Chicken & Rice Bake

Makes 4 servings

4 boneless, skinless chicken breast halves
    (about 1 pound)
1 jar (28 ounces) Ragú® Hearty Robust Blend
    Pasta Sauce
2 cups water
⅔ cup uncooked white rice
½ cup sliced pitted ripe olives
1 tablespoon capers, drained and chopped
1 teaspoon salt
½ teaspoon ground black pepper
¼ teaspoon dried oregano leaves, crushed
⅛ teaspoon crushed red pepper flakes

Preheat oven to 375°F. In 13×9-inch casserole,
combine all ingredients. Bake uncovered 40 minutes
or until rice is tender and chicken is no longer pink.

Fettuccine with Chunky
Feta-Tomato Sauce

Makes 6 servings

1 jar (28 ounces) Ragú® Chunky Gardenstyle
    Pasta Sauce
1 box (12 ounces) fettuccine, cooked and drained
8 ounces crumbled feta cheese (about 2 cups)
1 tablespoon finely chopped fresh parsley
    Pinch crushed red pepper flakes

In 2-quart saucepan, heat Ragú Chunky Gardenstyle
Pasta Sauce over low heat, stirring occasionally, until
heated through. Spoon sauce over hot fettuccine,
then sprinkle with cheese, parsley and red pepper
flakes.

Mediterranean Pasta & Chicken

Makes 4 servings

1 tablespoon olive or vegetable oil

8 ounces boneless, skinless chicken breasts, cut into thin strips

1 jar (28 ounces) Ragú® Chunky Gardenstyle Pasta Sauce

1 jar (7 ounces) roasted red peppers, drained and sliced

1 jar (6 ounces) marinated artichoke hearts, drained and coarsely chopped

⅔ cup sliced pitted ripe olives

¼ to ½ teaspoon crushed red pepper flakes

8 ounces rotelle or spiral pasta, cooked and drained

In 12-inch skillet, heat oil over medium-high heat and cook chicken, stirring frequently, 4 minutes or until no longer pink. Remove chicken and set aside.

In same skillet, stir in Ragú Chunky Gardenstyle Pasta Sauce, roasted peppers, artichokes, olives and red pepper flakes. Bring to a boil over high heat. Reduce heat to low and simmer uncovered, stirring occasionally, 10 minutes. Return chicken to skillet and heat through. Toss hot pasta with sauce and sprinkle, if desired, with grated Parmesan cheese.

Roasted Garlic
Swedish Meatballs

Makes 4 servings

1 pound ground beef
½ cup plain dry bread crumbs
1 egg
1 jar (17 ounces) Ragú® Cheese Creations!™
    Roasted Garlic Parmesan Pasta Sauce
1¼ cups beef broth
2 teaspoons Worcestershire sauce
1 teaspoon ground allspice (optional)

In large bowl, combine ground beef, bread crumbs and egg; shape into 20 (1½-inch) meatballs.

In 12-inch nonstick skillet, brown meatballs over medium-high heat.

Meanwhile, in medium bowl, combine Ragú Cheese Creations! Pasta Sauce, beef broth, Worcestershire sauce and allspice; stir into skillet. Bring to a boil over high heat. Reduce heat to low and simmer uncovered, stirring occasionally, 10 minutes or until meatballs are done and sauce is slightly thickened. Serve, if desired, over hot cooked noodles or rice.

Roasted Garlic
Swedish Meatballs

Classic Chicken Parmesan

Makes 6 servings

6 boneless, skinless chicken breast halves,
    pounded thin (about 1½ pounds)
2 eggs, slightly beaten
1 cup Italian seasoned dry bread crumbs
2 tablespoons olive or vegetable oil
1 jar (27.7 ounces) Ragú Old World Style®
    Pasta Sauce
1 cup shredded mozzarella cheese (about
    4 ounces)

Preheat oven to 375°F. Dip chicken in eggs, then bread crumbs, coating well.

In 12-inch skillet, heat oil over medium-high heat and brown chicken; drain on paper towels.

In 11×7-inch baking dish, evenly spread 1 cup Ragú Old World Style Pasta Sauce. Arrange chicken in dish, then top with remaining sauce. Sprinkle with mozzarella cheese and, if desired, grated Parmesan cheese. Bake 25 minutes or until chicken is no longer pink.

RECIPE TIP

To pound chicken, place a boneless, skinless breast between two sheets of waxed paper. Use a rolling pin to press down and out from the center to flatten.

Classic Chicken Parmesan

Cheddar Broccoli Soup

Makes 6 (1-cup) servings

1 tablespoon olive or vegetable oil
1 rib celery, chopped (about ½ cup)
1 carrot, chopped (about ½ cup)
1 small onion, chopped (about ½ cup)
½ teaspoon dried thyme leaves, crushed
    (optional)
2 cans (13¾ ounces each) chicken broth
1 jar (17 ounces) Ragú® Cheese Creations!™
    Double Cheddar Pasta Sauce
1 box (10 ounces) frozen chopped broccoli,
    thawed and drained

In 3-quart saucepan, heat oil over medium heat and cook celery, carrot, onion and thyme 3 minutes or until vegetables are almost tender. Add chicken broth and bring to a boil over high heat. Reduce heat to medium and simmer uncovered 10 minutes.

In food processor or blender, purée vegetable mixture until smooth; return to saucepan. Stir in Ragú Cheese Creations! Pasta Sauce and broccoli. Cook 10 minutes or until heated through.

Cheddar Broccoli Soup

Tortellini Carbonara

Makes 4 servings

1 package (15 ounces) cheese tortellini
1 box (10 ounces) frozen broccoli florets, thawed
1 jar (17 ounces) Ragú® Cheese Creations!™
  Roasted Garlic Parmesan Pasta Sauce
½ cup diced drained roasted red peppers
4 ounces bacon, crisp-cooked and crumbled

In 3-quart saucepan, cook tortellini according to package directions, adding broccoli during last 2 minutes of cooking; drain. Return pasta mixture to saucepan. Stir in Ragú Cheese Creations! Pasta Sauce and peppers. Turn onto platter and top with bacon. Garnish, if desired, with Parmesan cheese.

Linguine with Red Clam Sauce

Makes 8 servings

1 tablespoon olive or vegetable oil
2 cloves garlic, finely chopped
1 jar (27.7 ounces) Ragú Old World Style® Pasta
  Sauce
3 cans (6½ ounces each) minced clams, drained
  (reserve 1 cup liquid)
  Hot pepper sauce to taste (optional)
1 box (16 ounces) linguine, cooked and drained

In 2-quart saucepan, heat oil over low heat and cook garlic 30 seconds. Stir in Ragú Old World Style Pasta Sauce and reserved clam liquid; simmer 5 minutes. Stir in clams and hot pepper sauce; heat through. Spoon sauce over hot linguine.

Tortellini Carbonara

Penne Puttanesca

Makes 8 servings

3 tablespoons olive or vegetable oil
2 cloves garlic, finely chopped
1 jar (27.7 ounces) Ragú Old World Style®
   Pasta Sauce
¼ cup chopped pitted oil-cured olives
1 tablespoon capers, rinsed
½ teaspoon dried oregano leaves, crushed
¼ teaspoon crushed red pepper flakes
1 box (16 ounces) penne pasta, cooked, drained

In 12-inch skillet, heat oil over low heat and cook
garlic 30 seconds. Stir in remaining ingredients
except pasta. Simmer uncovered, stirring
occasionally, 15 minutes. Serve sauce over hot
pasta. Garnish, if desired, with chopped parsley.

Quick 'n Easy Pasta Bolognese

Makes 4 servings

½ pound ground beef
2 cloves garlic, finely chopped
1 jar (28 ounces) Ragú® Chunky Gardenstyle
   Pasta Sauce
¼ cup light cream or half-and-half
3 tablespoons dry white wine (optional)
8 ounces penne or ziti pasta, cooked and drained

In 12-inch skillet, brown ground beef with garlic over
medium-high heat; drain. Stir in Ragú Chunky
Gardenstyle Pasta Sauce, cream and wine. Simmer
uncovered, stirring occasionally, 15 minutes. Serve
over hot pasta and sprinkle, if desired, with grated
Parmesan cheese.

Fettuccine with Bacon-Tomato Sauce

Makes 6 servings

4 slices bacon, chopped
2 medium onions, thinly sliced
2 cloves garlic, finely chopped
1 jar (27.7 ounces) Ragú Old World Style®
    Pasta Sauce
2 tablespoons whipping or heavy cream
⅛ teaspoon crushed red pepper flakes
⅛ teaspoon ground black pepper
1 box (12 ounces) fettuccine, cooked and drained

In 12-inch skillet, cook bacon until crisp; reserve drippings. Add onions and garlic to reserved drippings and cook over medium heat, stirring occasionally, until onions are tender. Stir in Ragú Old World Style Pasta Sauce, cream, red pepper flakes and black pepper; heat through. To serve, toss sauce with hot fettuccine. Sprinkle, if desired, with grated Parmesan cheese.

RECIPE TIP

For a flavorful twist to this dish, substitute pancetta, an Italian bacon that is cured but not smoked, or prosciutto for the traditional bacon.

RAGÚ®

Sunday Suppers

Classic Stuffed Shells (page 30)

Classic Stuffed Shells

Makes 8 servings

1 jar (27.7 ounces) Ragú Old World Style®
   Pasta Sauce, divided
2 pounds part-skim ricotta cheese
2 cups part-skim shredded mozzarella cheese
   (about 8 ounces)
¼ cup grated Parmesan cheese
3 eggs
1 tablespoon finely chopped fresh parsley
⅛ teaspoon ground black pepper
1 box (12 ounces) jumbo shells pasta, cooked
   and drained

Preheat oven to 350°F. In 13×9-inch baking pan, evenly spread 1 cup Ragú Old World Style Pasta Sauce; set aside.

In large bowl, combine cheeses, eggs, parsley and black pepper. Fill shells with cheese mixture, then arrange in baking pan. Evenly top with remaining sauce. Bake 45 minutes or until sauce is bubbling.

RECIPE TIP

For a change of shape, substitute cooked and drained cannelloni or manicotti tubes for the jumbo shells. Use a teaspoon or pastry bag to fill the tubes from end to end, being careful not to overfill them.

Italian Vegetable Strata

Makes 6 servings

1 loaf Italian bread, cut into 1-inch slices
1 jar (28 ounces) Ragú® Chunky Gardenstyle
    Pasta Sauce
1½ cups shredded mozzarella cheese
1 zucchini, thinly sliced
1 jar (7 ounces) roasted red peppers packed in
    oil, drained
6 eggs, beaten
¼ cup grated Parmesan cheese

Preheat oven to 350°F. In greased 13×9-inch baking dish, arrange bread slices. In large bowl, combine Ragú Chunky Gardenstyle Pasta Sauce, mozzarella cheese, 1 cup water, vegetables, eggs and Parmesan cheese. Pour mixture over bread. Let stand 15 minutes. Bake covered 35 minutes or until vegetables are tender.

Baked Manicotti

Makes 4 servings

1 jar (27.7 ounces) Ragú Old World Style®
    Pasta Sauce
8 fresh or frozen prepared manicotti
½ cup shredded mozzarella cheese
2 tablespoons grated Parmesan cheese

Preheat oven to 450°F. In 13×9-inch baking dish, spread ½ of the Ragú Old World Style Pasta Sauce; arrange manicotti over sauce; top with remaining sauce. Sprinkle with cheeses. Bake covered 20 minutes. Remove cover and continue baking 5 minutes or until heated through.

Lasagna Florentine

Makes 8 servings

2 tablespoons olive or vegetable oil
3 medium carrots, finely chopped
1 package (8 to 10 ounces) sliced mushrooms
1 medium onion, finely chopped
2 cloves garlic, finely chopped
1 jar (28 ounces) Ragú® Hearty Robust Blend
   Pasta Sauce
1 container (15 ounces) ricotta cheese
2 cups shredded mozzarella cheese, divided
1 box (10 ounces) frozen chopped spinach,
   thawed and squeezed dry
¼ cup grated Parmesan cheese
2 eggs
1 teaspoon salt
1 teaspoon Italian seasoning
16 lasagna noodles, cooked and drained

Preheat oven to 375°F. In 12-inch skillet, heat oil over medium heat and cook carrots, mushrooms, onion and garlic until carrots are almost tender, about 5 minutes. Stir in Ragú Hearty Robust Blend Pasta Sauce; heat through. Meanwhile, in medium bowl, combine ricotta cheese, 1½ cups mozzarella cheese, spinach, Parmesan cheese, eggs, salt and Italian seasoning; set aside.

In 13×9-inch baking dish, evenly spread ½ cup sauce mixture. Arrange 4 lasagna noodles, lengthwise over sauce, overlapping edges slightly. Spread ⅓ of the ricotta mixture over noodles; repeat layers, ending with noodles. Top with remaining sauce and ½ cup mozzarella cheese. Cover with foil and bake 40 minutes. Remove foil and continue baking 10 minutes or until bubbling.

Lasagna Florentine

Pork Chops with Chili-Tomato Sauce

Makes 4 servings

- 4 bone-in or boneless pork chops, 1 inch thick
- 1 teaspoon salt, divided
- ¼ teaspoon ground black pepper
- 1 tablespoon olive or vegetable oil
- 2 red and/or green bell peppers, coarsely chopped
- 1 medium onion, chopped
- 1¼ cups Ragú® Chunky Gardenstyle Pasta Sauce
- ½ cup water
- ¼ cup apricot or peach preserves
- 1 tablespoon chili powder

Sprinkle chops with ½ teaspoon salt and black pepper. In 12-inch nonstick skillet, brown chops over medium-high heat. Remove chops and set aside.

In same skillet, heat oil over medium heat and cook bell peppers and onion, stirring occasionally, 2 minutes. Stir in Ragú Chunky Gardenstyle Pasta Sauce, water, preserves, chili powder and remaining ½ teaspoon salt. Bring to a boil over high heat. Reduce heat to low. Return chops to skillet, turning chops to coat. Simmer covered 8 minutes or until chops are tender. Serve, if desired, with hot cooked noodles or rice.

Pork Chop with Chili-Tomato Sauce

Stuffed Chicken Breasts with Hearty Tomato Sauce

Makes 4 servings

4 boneless, skinless chicken breast halves (about 1½ pounds)

4 ounces fontina or mozzarella cheese, cut into 4 equal slices

3 tablespoons drained and chopped oil-packed sun-dried tomatoes

¼ cup all-purpose flour

2 tablespoons olive or vegetable oil

2 cloves garlic, finely chopped

1½ cups Ragú® Hearty Robust Blend Pasta Sauce

¼ cup water

With knife parallel to cutting board, make 2-inch-long deep cut in center of each chicken breast half to form pocket. Evenly stuff pockets with cheese and sun-dried tomatoes; secure with wooden toothpicks. Sprinkle, if desired, with salt and pepper. Dip chicken breasts in flour.

In 12-inch skillet, heat oil over medium-high heat and brown chicken. Add garlic and cook, stirring occasionally, 30 seconds. Add Ragú Hearty Robust Blend Pasta Sauce and water and simmer covered 6 minutes or until chicken is no longer pink. Remove toothpicks. Serve, if desired, over hot steamed escarole or spinach.

Stuffed Chicken Breast with Hearty Tomato Sauce

Cheesy Chicken Pot Pie

Makes 6 servings

1 pound boneless, skinless chicken breast
    halves, cut into ½-inch chunks
1 tablespoon all-purpose flour
1 jar (17 ounces) Ragú® Cheese Creations!™
    Double Cheddar Pasta Sauce
1 bag (16 ounces) frozen mixed vegetables,
    thawed
1 prepared pastry for single-crust pie

Preheat oven to 425°F. In 2-quart casserole, toss chicken with flour. Stir in Ragú Cheese Creations! Pasta Sauce and vegetables. Cover casserole with prepared pastry. Press pastry around edge of casserole to seal; trim excess pastry, then flute edges. Cover with aluminum foil and bake 20 minutes. Remove foil and continue baking 20 minutes or until crust is golden and chicken is no longer pink. Let stand 5 minutes before serving.

RECIPE TIP

This is the perfect dish for leftovers. Substitute cooked pork roast, turkey breast or even roast beef for the chicken.

Cheesy Chicken Pot Pie

Hearty Lasagna Rolls

Makes 6 servings

1½ pounds ground beef
1 cup chopped fresh mushrooms
1 medium onion, finely chopped
1 small carrot, finely chopped
1 clove garlic, finely chopped
¼ cup dry red wine or beef broth
⅛ teaspoon cayenne pepper (optional)
2 cups shredded mozzarella cheese
1 egg, slightly beaten
5 tablespoons grated Parmesan cheese, divided
1 jar (28 ounces) Ragú® Hearty Robust Blend Pasta Sauce
12 ounces lasagna noodles, cooked and drained

Preheat oven to 350°F. In 12-inch skillet, brown ground beef over medium-high heat; drain. Stir in mushrooms, onion, carrot and garlic and cook over medium heat, stirring occasionally, until vegetables are tender. Stir in wine and cayenne pepper; cook over high heat 3 minutes. Remove from heat; let stand 10 minutes.

In medium bowl, thoroughly combine ground beef mixture, mozzarella cheese, egg and 2 tablespoons Parmesan cheese. In 13×9-inch baking dish, evenly pour 2 cups Ragú Hearty Robust Blend Pasta Sauce. Evenly spread ⅓ cup ground beef filling over each lasagna noodle. Carefully roll up noodles. Place seam-side-down in baking dish. Evenly spread remaining sauce over lasagna rolls. Bake covered 40 minutes. Sprinkle with remaining 3 tablespoons Parmesan cheese and bake uncovered 5 minutes or until bubbling.

Hearty Lasagna Rolls

Simmered Tuscan Chicken

Makes 6 servings

2 tablespoons olive or vegetable oil
1 pound boneless, skinless chicken breasts, cut
    into 1-inch cubes
2 cloves garlic, finely chopped
4 medium potatoes, cut into ½-inch cubes (about
    4 cups)
1 medium red bell pepper, cut into large pieces
1 jar (27.7 ounces) Ragú Old World Style®
    Pasta Sauce
1 pound fresh or frozen cut green beans
1 teaspoon dried basil leaves, crushed
    Salt and ground black pepper to taste

In 12-inch skillet, heat oil over medium-high heat and cook chicken with garlic until chicken is no longer pink. Remove chicken and set aside.

In same skillet, add potatoes and bell pepper. Cook over medium heat, stirring occasionally, 5 minutes. Stir in remaining ingredients. Bring to a boil over high heat. Reduce heat to low and simmer covered, stirring occasionally, 35 minutes or until potatoes are tender. Return chicken to skillet and heat through.

Simmered Tuscan Chicken

Mediterranean Pork with Olives

Makes 6 servings

1 tablespoon olive or vegetable oil
6 bone-in or boneless pork chops, ¾ inch thick
1 large onion, sliced
2 cloves garlic, finely chopped
¼ cup dry white wine
1 jar (27.7) Ragú Old World Style® Pasta Sauce
½ cup sliced pitted ripe olives
    Pinch ground cinnamon (optional)

In 12-inch skillet, heat oil over medium-high heat and brown chops. Remove and set aside.

In same skillet, cook onion and garlic over medium heat, stirring occasionally, until onion is tender. Add wine and bring to a boil over high heat, scraping brown bits from bottom of skillet. Return pork to skillet and stir in remaining ingredients. Simmer covered, stirring sauce occasionally, 20 minutes or until pork is tender. Serve, if desired, over hot cooked rice and garnish with fresh rosemary and additional olives.

RECIPE TIP

There are literally hundreds of varieties of olives. Experiment with different ones, including kalamata and niçoise. You'll be pleasantly surprised by the flavor differences.

Baked Eggplant Parmesan

Makes 6 servings

2 cups seasoned dry bread crumbs

1½ cups grated Parmesan cheese, divided

2 medium eggplants (about 2 pounds), peeled and cut into ¼-inch round slices

4 eggs, beaten with 3 tablespoons water

1 jar (28 ounces) Ragú® Hearty Robust Blend Pasta Sauce

1½ cups shredded mozzarella cheese (about 6 ounces)

Preheat oven to 350°F. In medium bowl, combine bread crumbs and ½ cup Parmesan cheese. Dip eggplant slices in egg mixture, then bread crumb mixture. On lightly oiled baking sheets, arrange eggplant slices in single layer; bake 25 minutes or until golden.

In 13×9-inch baking dish, evenly spread 1 cup Ragú Hearty Robust Blend Pasta Sauce. Layer ½ of the baked eggplant slices, then 1 cup sauce and ½ cup Parmesan cheese; repeat. Cover with aluminum foil and bake 45 minutes. Remove foil and sprinkle with mozzarella cheese. Bake uncovered an additional 10 minutes or until cheese is melted.

RAGÚ®

Casual
Entertaining

46

Chicken Puttanesca-Style (page 48)

Chicken Puttanesca-Style

Makes 4 servings

2 tablespoons olive or vegetable oil
1 (2½- to 3-pound) chicken, cut into pieces
1 medium onion, sliced
¼ cup balsamic vinegar
1 jar (27.7 ounces) Ragú Old World Style® Pasta Sauce
1 cup pitted ripe olives
1 tablespoon drained capers

In 12-inch skillet, heat oil over medium-high heat and brown chicken. Remove chicken and set aside; drain.

In same skillet, add onion and vinegar and cook over medium heat, stirring occasionally, 3 minutes. Stir in Ragú Old World Style Pasta Sauce. Return chicken to skillet and simmer covered 25 minutes or until chicken is no longer pink. Stir in olives and capers; heat through. Serve, if desired, over hot cooked rice and garnish with chopped fresh parsley.

RECIPE TIP

Be sure to use the best quality balsamic vinegar you can afford. In general, the longer it's been aged, the deeper and tastier the flavor.

Savory Potato & Roasted Garlic Soup

Makes 6 (1-cup) servings

2 slices bacon

1 pound all-purpose or red-skinned potatoes, peeled and cubed

1 medium onion, diced

1 small red bell pepper, diced

1 rib celery, chopped

¼ teaspoon dried thyme leaves, crushed

⅛ teaspoon ground black pepper

1 can (13¾ ounces) chicken broth

¼ cup dry white wine or chicken broth

1 jar (17 ounces) Ragú® Cheese Creations!™ Roasted Garlic Parmesan Pasta Sauce

In 3-quart saucepan, cook bacon; remove and crumble. Reserve drippings. Add potatoes, onion, bell pepper, celery, thyme and black pepper to reserved drippings. Cook over medium heat, stirring occasionally, 6 minutes or until onion is tender. Stir in chicken broth and wine. Bring to a boil over high heat. Reduce heat to low and simmer covered 10 minutes or until vegetables are tender. Stir in Ragú Cheese Creations! Pasta Sauce; heat through. Garnish with bacon.

Hearty Beef Bourguignonne

Makes 4 servings

4 slices bacon, chopped
1 medium onion, chopped
1 large carrot, chopped
2 pounds boneless sirloin steak, cut into ¾-inch cubes
½ cup dry red wine or beef broth
1 jar (28 ounces) Ragú® Hearty Robust Blend Pasta Sauce

In 6-quart saucepan or Dutch oven, cook bacon over medium heat, stirring occasionally, 4 minutes or until crisp. Stir in onion and carrot and cook, stirring occasionally, 5 minutes. Stir in steak and cook over medium-high heat, stirring occasionally, 5 minutes or until steak is no longer pink. Add wine and Ragú Hearty Robust Blend Pasta Sauce; bring to a boil over high heat. Reduce heat to low and simmer covered, stirring occasionally, 30 minutes. Serve, if desired, with hot cooked rice or noodles.

RECIPE TIP

If cooking with wine, use the quality of wine which you would also enjoy drinking. For this classic dinner—your best Burgundy!

Hearty Beef Bourguignonne

Roasted Garlic Parmesan Penne Primavera

Makes 8 servings

1 box (16 ounces) penne pasta
1 medium carrot, cut into very thin strips
1 cup snow peas
1 small red bell pepper, cut into very thin strips
1 jar (17 ounces) Ragú® Cheese Creations!™
   Roasted Garlic Parmesan Pasta Sauce
½ cup chicken broth
⅛ teaspoon ground black pepper
⅛ teaspoon ground nutmeg (optional)

Cook pasta according to package directions, adding vegetables during last 3 minutes of cooking; drain. Return to saucepan and stir in Ragú Cheese Creations! Pasta Sauce, chicken broth, black pepper and nutmeg; heat through. Sprinkle, if desired, with grated Parmesan cheese.

RECIPE TIP

To reheat leftovers (as if there'll be any!), microwave in a covered dish on High (100% power) for about 1 minute. If not heated through, stir and continue cooking, checking at 15 second intervals.

Roasted Garlic Parmesan Penne Primavera

Southwestern Fettuccine

Makes 4 servings

1 tablespoon vegetable oil
1 medium red bell pepper, thinly sliced
1 jar (17 ounces) Ragú® Cheese Creations!™
  Spicy Cheddar & Tomato Pasta Sauce
1 box (10 ounces) frozen whole kernel corn,
  thawed
1 box (12 ounces) fettuccine, cooked and drained

In 12-inch skillet, heat oil over medium heat and cook bell pepper until tender. Stir in Ragú Cheese Creations! Pasta Sauce and corn. Simmer uncovered, stirring occasionally, 10 minutes. Spoon over hot fettuccine and garnish, if desired, with cilantro.

Ragú® Steak Pizzaiola

Makes 4 servings

4 eye-round steaks (1½ pounds)
2 tablespoons finely chopped garlic
¼ cup grated Parmesan cheese, divided
½ teaspoon salt
½ teaspoon ground black pepper
2 cups frozen French-cut green beans, thawed
1 jar (28 ounces) Ragú® Hearty Robust Blend
  Pasta Sauce

Preheat oven to 400°F. On bottom of 13×9-inch baking pan, arrange steaks. Sprinkle steaks with garlic, ½ of the Parmesan cheese, salt and pepper. Add green beans and Ragú Hearty Robust Blend Pasta Sauce. Bake 20 minutes or until desired doneness. Sprinkle with remaining cheese.

Southwestern Fettuccine

Sausage & Red Pepper Risotto

Makes 4 main-dish or 8 side-dish servings

4½ cups chicken broth

  8 ounces sweet Italian sausage links, removed
      from casing

  1 tablespoon olive or vegetable oil

  1 large onion, chopped

  1 medium red bell pepper, chopped

  1 clove garlic, finely chopped

1½ cups arborio or regular rice

 ⅓ cup dry white wine or chicken broth

 ⅛ teaspoon dried oregano leaves, crushed

  1 cup Ragú® Light Pasta Sauce

 ¼ cup grated Parmesan cheese

 ⅛ teaspoon ground black pepper

In 2-quart saucepan, heat chicken broth; set aside.

In heavy-duty 3-quart saucepan, brown sausage over medium-high heat 4 minutes or until sausage is no longer pink; remove sausage. In same 3-quart saucepan, add oil and cook onion over medium heat, stirring occasionally, 3 minutes. Stir in bell pepper and garlic and cook 1 minute. Add rice and cook, stirring occasionally, 1 minute. Slowly add 1 cup broth, wine and oregano and cook, stirring constantly, until liquid is absorbed. Continue adding 2 cups broth, 1 cup at a time, stirring frequently, until liquid is absorbed.

Meanwhile, stir Ragú Light Pasta Sauce into remaining 1½ cups broth; heat through. Continue adding broth mixture, 1 cup at a time, stirring frequently, until rice is slightly creamy and just tender. Return sausage to saucepan and stir in cheese and black pepper. Serve immediately.

Sausage & Red Pepper Risotto

Savory Veal Ragú®

Makes 4 servings

1 tablespoon olive or vegetable oil
2 pounds veal shoulder, cubed
2 green or red bell peppers, sliced
1 small onion, chopped
2 ribs celery, chopped
2 carrots, chopped
2 cloves garlic, finely chopped
1 jar (27.7 ounces) Ragú Old World Style®
 Pasta Sauce
½ cup water
¼ cup Burgundy wine
½ teaspoon salt

Preheat oven to 350°F. In 6-quart Dutch oven, heat oil and brown veal in two batches. Return veal to Dutch oven. Stir in bell peppers, onion, celery, carrots and garlic and cook 5 minutes. Stir in Ragú Old World Style Pasta Sauce, water, wine and salt. Bake covered 1 hour. Remove cover and stir. Continue baking uncovered 30 minutes or until veal and vegetables are tender.

Chicken Cacciatore

Makes 4 servings

1 tablespoon olive or vegetable oil
1 small green bell pepper, sliced
1 small onion, sliced
½ teaspoon garlic powder
1 pound boneless, skinless chicken breast halves
3 tablespoons sherry
¼ teaspoon ground black pepper
1 jar (27.7 ounces) Ragú Old World Style® Pasta Sauce

In 12-inch skillet, heat oil over medium heat and cook bell pepper, onion and garlic powder about 3 minutes or until vegetables are crisp-tender. Add chicken and brown 3 minutes. Stir in sherry and black pepper; cook 3 minutes. Stir in Ragú Old World Style Pasta Sauce and cook over low heat 8 minutes or until chicken is no longer pink. Serve over hot cooked rice or pasta.

RECIPE TIP

Italian for "hunter", cacciatore sauce is also excellent on pasta, pork chops and pan-fried steaks.

*Vegetable-Stuffed
Baked Potato (page 62)*

Vegetable-Stuffed Baked Potatoes

Makes 6 servings

1 jar (17 ounces) Ragú® Cheese Creations!™
  Roasted Garlic Parmesan Pasta Sauce or
  Double Cheddar Pasta Sauce
1 bag (16 ounces) frozen assorted vegetables,
  cooked and drained
6 large baking potatoes, unpeeled and baked

In 2-quart saucepan, heat Ragú Cheese Creations!
Pasta Sauce. Stir in vegetables; heat through.

Cut a lengthwise slice from top of each potato.
Lightly mash pulp in each potato. Evenly spoon
sauce mixture onto each potato. Sprinkle, if desired,
with ground black pepper.

Easy Sloppy Joes

Makes 8 servings

1 pound ground beef
1 medium onion, chopped
2 cups Ragú® Hearty Robust Blend Pasta Sauce
2 tablespoons sweet relish
1 tablespoon chili powder
6 toasted rolls or hamburger buns

In 12-inch skillet, brown ground beef with onion over
medium-high heat; drain. Stir in remaining
ingredients except rolls. Simmer uncovered, stirring
occasionally, 15 minutes. Serve on rolls.

Beefy Mac & Double Cheddar

Makes 4 servings

    1 pound ground beef
3½ cups water
    2 cups elbow macaroni
    1 jar (17 ounces) Ragú® Cheese Creations!™
        Double Cheddar Pasta Sauce

In 12-inch skillet, brown ground beef; drain. Remove from skillet and set aside.

In same skillet, bring water to a boil over high heat. Stir in macaroni and cook 6 minutes or until tender. Return ground beef to skillet. Stir in Ragú Cheese Creations! Pasta Sauce; heat through. Season, if desired, with salt and ground black pepper.

Three Cheese Pasta

Makes 8 servings

    1 box (16 ounces) rotini or radiatore pasta,
        cooked and drained
    1 cup shredded mozzarella cheese (about
        4 ounces)
    1 cup shredded fontina and/or provolone cheese
        (about 4 ounces)
¼ cup grated Parmesan cheese
    1 jar (27.7 ounces) Ragú Old World Style® Pasta
        Sauce, heated to boiling

In medium bowl, toss hot pasta, cheeses and Ragú Old World Style Pasta Sauce. Sprinkle, if desired, with chopped fresh parsley.

Spicy Cheddar & Chicken Burritos

Makes 8 burritos

1 jar (17 ounces) Ragú® Cheese Creations!™ Spicy Cheddar & Tomato Pasta Sauce, divided
1 can (15 ounces) black beans or red kidney beans, rinsed and drained
8 ounces shredded cooked chicken
1 cup cooked rice
8 (8-inch) flour tortillas
⅓ cup shredded cheddar cheese (about 2 ounces)

Preheat oven to 350°F. In large bowl, combine 1¼ cups Ragú Cheese Creations! Pasta Sauce, beans, chicken and rice. Evenly spoon ½ cup chicken mixture onto tortillas, then roll. In 11×7-inch baking dish sprayed with nonstick cooking spray, arrange tortillas; top with remaining Pasta Sauce. Cover with aluminum foil and bake 15 minutes. Remove foil and sprinkle with cheese. Continue baking 5 minutes or until cheese is melted and tortillas are heated through. Serve, if desired, with shredded lettuce, sour cream and guacamole.

Spicy Cheddar & Chicken Burritos

Cheddar Burger Mashed Potato Bake

Makes 8 servings

2 pounds ground beef

1 medium onion, chopped

1 jar (17 ounces) Ragú® Cheese Creations!™ Double Cheddar Pasta Sauce

2 teaspoons dry mustard

4 cups prepared mashed potatoes

Preheat oven to 425°F. In 12-inch skillet, brown ground beef over medium-high heat; drain. Add onion and cook, stirring occasionally, 2 minutes. Stir in Ragú Cheese Creations! Pasta Sauce, mustard and, if desired, salt and ground black pepper to taste. Simmer uncovered, stirring occasionally, 3 minutes or until heated through.

Turn into 2-quart casserole; evenly top with mashed potatoes. Bake 25 minutes or until potatoes are lightly golden.

RECIPE TIP

When making mashed potatoes, use Idaho or all-purpose potatoes for marvelous flavor and texture. Heat the milk before adding it—this minimizes any starchiness.

Cheddar Burger Mashed Potato Bake

Fiesta Chicken Nachos

Makes 4 servings

1 tablespoon olive or vegetable oil
1 pound boneless, skinless chicken breasts
1 jar (17 ounces) Ragú® Cheese Creations!™
    Spicy Cheddar & Tomato Pasta Sauce
1 bag (9 ounces) tortilla chips
2 green and/or red bell peppers, diced
1 small onion, chopped
1 large tomato, diced

In 12-inch skillet, heat oil over medium-high heat and cook chicken, stirring occasionally, 8 minutes or until no longer pink. Remove from skillet; cut into strips.

In same skillet, combine chicken and Ragú Cheese Creations! Pasta Sauce; heat through.

On serving platter, arrange layer of tortilla chips, then ½ of the sauce mixture, bell peppers, onion and tomato; repeat, ending with tomato. Garnish, if desired, with chopped fresh cilantro and shredded lettuce.

RECIPE TIP

For a spicier dish, add chopped jalapeño peppers or hot pepper sauce to suit your taste.

Fiesta Chicken Nachos

Ragú® Chili

Makes 8 servings

2 pounds ground beef
1 large onion, chopped
2 cloves garlic, finely chopped
1 jar (28 ounces) Ragú® Hearty Robust Blend
    Pasta Sauce
1 can (15 ounces) red kidney beans, rinsed and
    drained
2 tablespoons chili powder

In 12-inch skillet, brown ground beef with onion and garlic over medium-high heat; drain. Stir in remaining ingredients. (For spicier Ragú Chili, stir in ½ teaspoon each ground cumin and dried oregano.) Simmer uncovered, stirring occasionally, 20 minutes. Serve, if desired, with shredded Cheddar cheese.

Pepperoni Pasta Ruffles

Makes 8 servings

1 tablespoon olive or vegetable oil
2 red and/or green bell peppers, diced
1 jar (27.7 ounces) Ragú Old World Style® Pasta
    Sauce
1 package (3½ ounces) sliced pepperoni, halved
8 ounces mozzarella cheese, diced
1 box (16 ounces) fusilli or rotini pasta, cooked
    and drained

In 12-inch skillet, heat oil over medium heat and cook bell peppers 3 minutes or until tender. Stir in Ragú Old World Style Pasta Sauce and simmer uncovered, stirring occasionally, 10 minutes. Toss sauce, pepperoni and cheese with hot pasta.

French Bread Florentine

Makes 4 servings

¾ pound hot or sweet Italian sausage links,
   removed from casing and crumbled

⅓ cup chopped onion

1 loaf French bread (about 12 inches long),
   halved lengthwise

1 cup Ragú Pizza Quick® Sauce

1 box (10 ounces) frozen chopped spinach,
   thawed and squeezed dry

1 cup shredded mozzarella cheese (about
   4 ounces)

Preheat oven to 375°F. In 10-inch nonstick skillet, brown sausage with onion over medium-high heat until sausage is no longer pink.

On baking sheet, arrange bread halves. Evenly spread Ragú Pizza Quick Sauce on bread halves, then top with sausage mixture, then spinach and cheese. Bake 20 minutes or until cheese is melted.

RECIPE TIP

These sausage-spinach pizzas are great for parties and after-school snacks. Cut them into 2-inch pieces to fit kid-size mouths.

On the Lighter Side

Vegetable Bow Tie Pasta (page 74)

Vegetable Bow Tie Pasta

Makes 6 servings

1 box (16 ounces) bow tie pasta
1 cup chopped fresh broccoli
1 cup shredded carrots
1 small red bell pepper, diced
1 small zucchini or yellow squash, diced
1 jar (27.5 ounces) Ragú® Light Pasta Sauce

Cook pasta according to package directions, stirring in vegetables during last 5 minutes of boiling; drain.

In 2-quart saucepan, heat Ragú Light Pasta Sauce. Toss sauce with hot pasta and sprinkle, if desired, with grated Parmesan cheese.

NUTRITION INFORMATION PER SERVING

Calories 380
Protein . . . . 14 g
Carbohydrate . . . . 76 g
Fat . . . . 2 g
Sodium . . . . 430 mg
Cholesterol . . . . 0 mg

Fettuccine with Turkey Bolognese Sauce

Makes 6 servings

1 teaspoon olive or vegetable oil
2 carrots, chopped
1 small onion, chopped
1 rib celery, chopped
1 to 1½ pounds lean ground turkey
¼ cup dry red wine or chicken broth
1 jar (27.5 ounces) Ragú® Light Pasta Sauce
2 tablespoons chopped fresh parsley
1 box (16 ounces) fettuccine, cooked and drained

In 12-inch nonstick skillet, heat oil over medium heat and cook carrots, onion and celery, stirring frequently, 5 minutes or until tender. Add turkey and cook, breaking up with spoon, until turkey is no longer pink. Stir in wine. Bring to a boil over high heat. Reduce heat to low and simmer uncovered 3 minutes. Stir in Ragú Light Pasta Sauce and parsley; simmer, stirring occasionally, 5 minutes. Season, if desired, with salt and ground black pepper. Serve over hot fettuccine.

NUTRITION INFORMATION PER SERVING

Calories	500
Protein	26 g
Carbohydrate	75 g
Fat	9 g
Sodium	520 mg
Cholesterol	60 mg

Summer Minestrone with Pesto

Makes 8 (1-cup) servings

4 tablespoons olive or vegetable oil, divided
2 cups diced carrots
3 medium zucchini and/or yellow squash, diced
1 jar (27.5 ounces) Ragú® Light Pasta Sauce
2 cans (13¾ ounces each) chicken or vegetable broth
1 can (19 ounces) cannellini or white kidney beans, rinsed and drained
1 cup packed fresh basil leaves
1 large clove garlic, finely chopped
¼ teaspoon salt

In 5-quart saucepan, heat 1 tablespoon oil over medium-high heat and cook carrots and zucchini, stirring occasionally, 8 minutes. Stir in Ragú Light Pasta Sauce and chicken broth. Bring to a boil over high heat. Reduce heat to low and simmer covered, stirring occasionally, 20 minutes or until vegetables are tender. Stir in beans; heat through.

Meanwhile, for pesto, in blender or food processor, process basil, garlic, salt and remaining 3 tablespoons oil until basil is finely chopped. To serve, ladle soup into bowls and garnish each with spoonful of pesto.

NUTRITION INFORMATION PER SERVING

	SOUP	PESTO
Calories	160	49
Protein	8 g	0 g
Carbohydrate	26 g	0 g
Fat	2.5 g	5 g
Sodium	480 mg	72.5 mg
Cholesterol	0 mg	0 mg

Summer Minestrone with Pesto

Eggplant & Shrimp over Fusilli

Makes 6 servings

2 tablespoons olive or vegetable oil, divided
1 large eggplant, peeled and diced
⅔ cup water, divided
1 medium onion, chopped
2 cloves garlic, finely chopped
¾ teaspoon salt
¼ teaspoon ground black pepper
1 jar (27.5 ounces) Ragú® Light Pasta Sauce
8 ounces uncooked shrimp, peeled and deveined
16 ounces fusilli pasta, cooked and drained
1 cup crumbled feta cheese (optional)

In 12-inch nonstick skillet, heat 1 tablespoon oil over medium heat and cook eggplant with ⅓ cup water, covered, stirring occasionally, 15 minutes or until eggplant is tender. Remove eggplant and set aside.

In same skillet, heat remaining 1 tablespoon oil over medium heat and cook onion, garlic, salt and pepper 2 minutes or until onion is tender. Stir in Ragú Light Pasta Sauce, remaining ⅓ cup water and eggplant. Reduce heat to low and simmer covered, stirring occasionally, 6 minutes. Stir in shrimp and simmer, stirring occasionally, 4 minutes or until shrimp turn pink. Serve over hot pasta and sprinkle with crumbled feta cheese.

NUTRITION INFORMATION PER SERVING

Calories	400
Protein	17 g
Carbohydrate	69 g
Fat	7 g
Sodium	760 mg
Cholesterol	45 mg

Eggplant & Shrimp over Fusilli

Moroccan-Style Chicken over Couscous

Makes 4 servings

4 boneless, skinless chicken thighs (about
    1¼ pounds)
1 teaspoon olive or vegetable oil
2 cloves garlic, finely chopped
1 tablespoon lemon juice
1 jar (27.5 ounces) Ragú® Light Pasta Sauce
1 tablespoon chopped cilantro (optional)
½ teaspoon finely grated lemon peel (optional)
1 box (10 ounces) couscous, cooked according
    to package directions

Season chicken, if desired, with salt and ground black pepper.

In 12-inch skillet, heat oil over medium-high heat and brown chicken. Add garlic and cook 30 seconds. Stir in lemon juice and cook over medium heat, stirring occasionally, 4 minutes. Stir in Ragú Light Pasta Sauce, cilantro and lemon peel. Bring to a boil over high heat. Reduce heat to low and simmer covered, stirring occasionally, 10 minutes or until chicken is no longer pink. Serve over hot couscous.

NUTRITION INFORMATION PER SERVING

Calories	470
Protein	26 g
Carbohydrate	72 g
Fat	8 g
Sodium	680 mg
Cholesterol	50 mg

Pork & Pepper Enchiladas

Makes 6 servings

2 teaspoons olive or vegetable oil, divided

¾ pound center cut boneless pork loin, cut into
thin strips

3 red, yellow and/or green bell peppers, cut into
thin strips

1 medium onion, sliced

1 tablespoon finely chopped garlic

1 tablespoon lime juice

1 jar (27.5 ounces) Ragú® Light Pasta Sauce,
divided

6 (6-inch) flour tortillas, heated

½ cup shredded cheddar cheese (about
2 ounces)

In 12-inch nonstick skillet, heat 1 teaspoon oil over
medium-high heat and brown pork 4 minutes.
Remove and set aside.

In same skillet, heat remaining 1 teaspoon oil over
medium heat and cook bell peppers and onion 9
minutes or until tender. Return pork to skillet; add
garlic and cook 1 minute. Stir in lime juice and ½
cup Ragú Light Pasta Sauce; heat through.

Fill each tortilla with ½ cup pork mixture and evenly
sprinkle with cheese; roll up. Heat remaining pasta
sauce and serve over enchiladas.

NUTRITION INFORMATION PER SERVING

Calories	250
Protein	16 g
Carbohydrate	28 g
Fat	9 g
Sodium	450 mg
Cholesterol	35 mg

Snacks & Sides

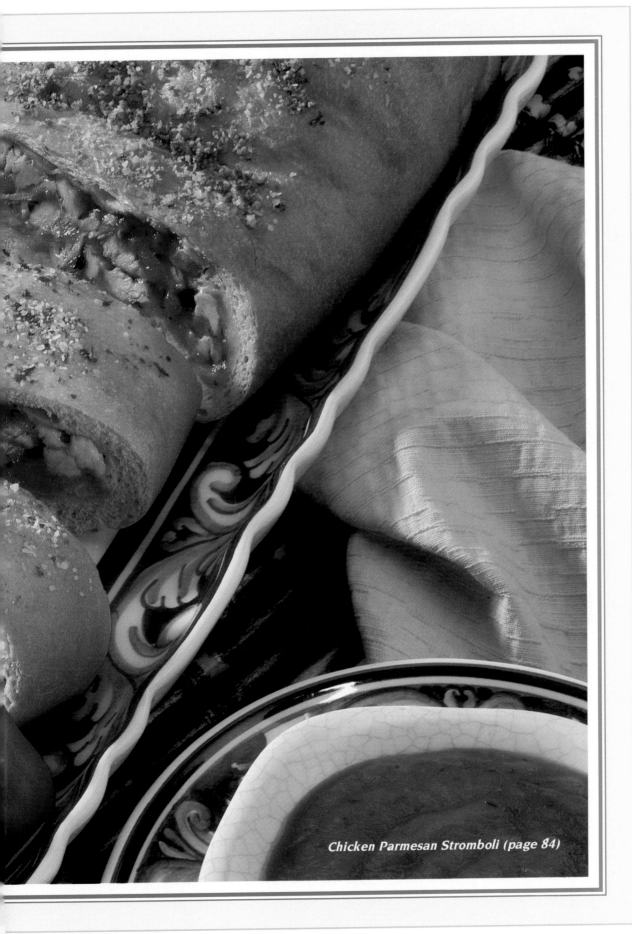

Chicken Parmesan Stromboli (page 84)

Chicken Parmesan Stromboli

Makes 6 servings

1 pound boneless, skinless chicken breast halves
½ teaspoon salt
¼ teaspoon ground black pepper
2 teaspoons olive or vegetable oil
2 cups shredded mozzarella cheese (about
    8 ounces)
1 jar (28 ounces) Ragú® Chunky Gardenstyle
    Pasta Sauce, divided
2 tablespoons grated Parmesan cheese
1 tablespoon finely chopped fresh parsley
1 pound fresh or thawed frozen bread dough

Preheat oven to 400°F. Season chicken with salt and pepper. In 12-inch skillet, heat oil over medium-high heat and brown chicken. Remove chicken from skillet and let cool; pull into large shreds.

In medium bowl, combine chicken, mozzarella cheese, ½ cup Ragú Chunky Gardenstyle Pasta Sauce, Parmesan cheese and parsley; set aside.

On greased jelly-roll pan, press dough to form 12×10-inch rectangle. Arrange chicken mixture down center of dough. Cover filling bringing one long side into center, then overlap with the other long side; pinch seam to seal. Fold in ends and pinch to seal. Arrange on pan, seam-side down. Gently press in sides to form 12×4-inch loaf. Bake 35 minutes or until dough is cooked and golden. Cut stromboli into slices. Heat remaining pasta sauce and serve with stromboli.

Cajun Shrimp Wraps

Makes 8 servings

½ cup uncooked rice
1 tablespoon olive or vegetable oil
1 pound uncooked medium shrimp, peeled and
    deveined
1 small red onion, chopped
1 tablespoon finely chopped garlic
2 teaspoons Cajun seasoning (optional)
1 cup Ragú Old World Style® Pasta Sauce
8 (8-inch) flour tortillas, warmed

Cook rice according to package directions.

Meanwhile, in 12-inch skillet, heat oil over medium-high heat and cook shrimp, onion, garlic and Cajun seasoning 3 minutes or until shrimp turn pink. Stir in Ragú Old World Style Pasta Sauce; heat through. Stir hot cooked rice into shrimp mixture. Spoon ½ cup filling onto each tortilla; roll and serve.

RECIPE TIP

To peel and devein shrimp, start at the head of the shrimp and use your fingers to peel off the shell. Use a sharp knife to slit the back and lift out the dark vein.

Mushroom Parmesan Crostini

Makes 12 crostini

1 tablespoon olive or vegetable oil
1 clove garlic, finely chopped
1 cup chopped mushrooms
1 loaf Italian or French bread (about 12 inches long), cut into 12 slices and toasted
¾ cup Ragú Pizza Quick® Sauce
¼ cup grated Parmesan cheese
1 tablespoon finely chopped fresh basil leaves or 1 teaspoon dried basil leaves

Preheat oven to 375°F. In 8-inch nonstick skillet, heat oil over medium heat and cook garlic 30 seconds. Add mushrooms and cook, stirring occasionally, 2 minutes or until liquid evaporates.

On baking sheet, arrange bread slices. Evenly spread Ragú Pizza Quick Sauce on bread slices, then top with mushroom mixture, cheese and basil. Bake 15 minutes or until heated through.

RECIPE TIP

Many varieties of wild mushrooms are available in supermarkets and specialty grocery stores. Shiitake, portobello and cremini mushrooms all have excellent flavor.

Mushroom Parmesan Crostini

Pizza Primavera

Makes 4 servings

¾ cup Ragú Pizza Quick® Sauce
1 (10-inch) prebaked pizza crust
1 medium red bell pepper, thinly sliced
1 cup sliced zucchini
½ cup chopped red onion
1 cup shredded mozzarella cheese (about
    4 ounces)

Preheat oven to 450°F. Evenly spread Ragú Pizza
Quick Sauce on pizza crust, then top with remaining
ingredients. Bake 12 minutes or until cheese is
melted.

Roasted Garlic Mashed Potatoes

Makes 12 servings

3 pounds all-purpose potatoes, peeled, if desired,
    and cut into chunks
1 jar (17 ounces) Ragú® Cheese Creations!™
    Roasted Garlic Parmesan Pasta Sauce
¼ cup chopped fresh parsley (optional)
½ teaspoon salt
¼ teaspoon ground black pepper

In 3-quart saucepan, cover potatoes with water.
Bring to a boil over high heat. Reduce heat to low
and simmer uncovered 20 minutes or until potatoes
are very tender; drain. Return potatoes to saucepan;
mash potatoes with Ragú Cheese Creations! Pasta
Sauce, parsley, salt and pepper.

Pizza Primavera

Tuscan-Style Sausage Sandwiches

Makes 4 servings

1 pound hot or sweet Italian sausage links, sliced
1 box (10 ounces) frozen chopped spinach, thawed and squeezed dry
1 small onion, sliced
½ cup fresh or drained canned sliced mushrooms
1 jar (28 ounces) Ragú® Hearty Robust Blend Pasta Sauce
1 loaf Italian or French bread (about 16 inches long), cut into 4 rolls

In 12-inch skillet, brown sausage over medium-high heat. Stir in spinach, onion and mushrooms. Cook, stirring occasionally, 5 minutes or until sausage is done. Stir in Ragú Hearty Robust Blend Pasta Sauce; heat through.

For each sandwich, split open each roll and evenly spoon in sausage mixture. Sprinkle, if desired, with crushed red pepper flakes.

RECIPE TIP

These sausages can also be grilled. Combine your favorite Ragú Pasta Sauce with mustard, vinegar and extra-virgin olive oil for an exciting marinade.

Tuscan-Style Sausage Sandwich

Potato 'n Onion Bake

Makes 4 servings

1 pound all-purpose or baking potatoes, thinly
   sliced
2 medium onions, thinly sliced
2 tablespoons olive or vegetable oil
½ teaspoon salt
½ teaspoon ground black pepper
2 cups Ragú® Chunky Gardenstyle Pasta Sauce
3 tablespoons grated Parmesan cheese

Preheat oven to 400°F. In 2-quart baking dish, layer
½ each of the potatoes, onions, oil, salt and pepper;
repeat layer. Bake covered 20 minutes or until
potatoes are tender. Remove cover; pour Ragú
Chunky Gardenstyle Pasta Sauce over potato
mixture; sprinkle with Parmesan cheese. Bake an
additional 10 minutes or until heated through.

Zesty Cheddar Bean Dip

Makes 2 cups dip

1 can (15 ounces) black beans, rinsed and
   drained
1 cup Ragú® Cheese Creations!™ Spicy Cheddar
   & Tomato Pasta Sauce
1 can (4½ ounces) chopped green chilies,
   drained
1 green onion, chopped
1 tablespoon chopped cilantro

In microwavable bowl, mash beans. Stir in remaining
ingredients. Heat in microwave until warm. Serve
with tortilla chips.

Index

INDEX